ISBN 978-0-332-58161-3
PIBN 11242585

Forgotten Books is a registered trademark of FB &c Ltd.
Copyright © 2018 FB &c Ltd.
FB &c Ltd, Dalton House, 60 Windsor Avenue, London, SW19 2RR.
Company number 08720141. Registered in England and Wales.

For support please visit www.forgottenbooks.com

1 MONTH OF
FREE
READING

at

www.ForgottenBooks.com

By purchasing this book you are eligible for one month membership to ForgottenBooks.com, giving you unlimited access to our entire collection of over 1,000,000 titles via our web site and mobile apps.

To claim your free month visit:

www.forgottenbooks.com/free1242585

English
Français
Deutsche
Italiano
Español
Português

www.forgottenbooks.com

Mythology Photography **Fiction**
Fishing Christianity **Art** Cooking
Essays Buddhism Freemasonry
Medicine **Biology** Music **Ancient
Egypt** Evolution Carpentry Physics
Dance Geology **Mathematics** Fitness
Shakespeare **Folklore** Yoga Marketing
Confidence Immortality Biographies
Poetry **Psychology** Witchcraft
Electronics Chemistry History **Law**
Accounting **Philosophy** Anthropology
Alchemy Drama Quantum Mechanics
Atheism Sexual Health **Ancient History**
Entrepreneurship Languages Sport
Paleontology Needlework Islam
Metaphysics Investment Archaeology
Parenting Statistics Criminology
Motivational

BULLETIN OF THE UNIVERSITY OF WISCONSIN
No. 947; High School Series, No. 18

A FOUR YEAR COURSE IN FRENCH FOR HIGH SCHOOLS

PREPARED BY

BARRY CERF

Associate Professor of Romance Languages
The University of Wisconsin

The University of Wisconsin
MADISON
July, 1918

PREFACE

The following outline of a four year high school course in French is offered merely as a guide; suggestions of improvements that may occur to any teacher will be gratefully received.

In all large high schools it is hoped that a four year course in French will be established and maintained. The value of the study of French is being fully recognized at the present time. It is the key to one of the richest literatures in the world. It is the language most widely used with the exception of English. It is generally written and spoken as the second language in all of South America (the Spanish countries as well as Brazil),—almost everywhere throughout the world, in fact, where its place is not taken by English. Under these circumstances a grave duty devolves upon the teacher of French, a duty which he must strive to his utmost to meet.

The Department of Romance Languages of the University of Wisconsin will try to answer all inquiries which teachers of the state may submit to it, and hopes that teachers will consider that high school and University instructors of French form one coordinated whole.

The compiler of this bulletin desires to thank the many teachers who have aided him, especially Miss Laura Johnson, of the Wisconsin High School, Madison, and Professor C. E. Cousins of the University of Wisconsin.

A FOUR YEAR COURSE IN FRENCH FOR HIGH SCHOOLS

Method. The aim of the high school course is to prepare the pupil to read French easily, to speak and write it with some degree of fluency.

There can be no doubt that the present tendency in modern language instruction is toward a modified form of the so-called Direct Method and its derivative variations. The following sections will show sufficiently what type of modification is adopted in this bulletin.

The first difficulty the teacher will have to meet is the apportionment of the recitation period best calculated to achieve the aim stated above. In general, it seems desirable to devote at least a third of the time to translation and at least a third to oral drill. The remaining third may be given to correcting sentences written on the board, reading the French, translation, etc., but these exercises may well be restricted to much less than a third of the time, or, indeed, entirely eliminated during a large part of the year's work and the time thus saved allotted to translation and oral drill.

II

Pronunciation. A reasonably correct pronunciation is essential and can be acquired only by persistent effort on the part of the teacher during the whole first year.

Delay in taking up this important matter is often disastrous. The first day should be devoted to an explanation of the French sounds. If the teacher has had long experience, he may trust his ability to control the imitative faculty of his pupils, but in the vast majority of cases, better progress will be realized and much time will be saved by the use of the approximate equivalents found in English (e. g.

é = a in mate, è = e in met). Some teachers avoid English
key-words and rely on physiological explanations of the for-
mation of sounds; the results attained do not, however,
justify the loss of time and the bewilderment of the pupil
occasioned by the use of this method. But, in the case of
the so-called rounded front vowels (pur, peu, peur) for
which there are no corresponding English sounds, explanation must be resorted to: for pur pronounce the vowel in
vite and round the lips to the whistling position; for peu
pronounce the vowel in blé and round the lips to the
whistling position; for peur pronounce the eu in peu with
the mouth a little more open. It is not wise to insist upon
the distinction between peu and peur during the first few
months: pronounce both sounds like u in English burr;
likewise, for the first few months ou and i may be given full
vocalic sound in words like louer and ciel which are nor-
mally monosyllabic.

It is certainly not desirable during the first year to try
to distinguish between English and French consonantal
sounds, except that, where possible, pupils should be made
to pronounce some kind of r and should be made to sound
fully final stop consonants (occlusion and explosion; not
merely occlusion as in English).   ·

There can be no doubt that a phonetic alphabet is of
great value in clarifying explanations and in affording the
pupil a check on his pronunciation while he is studying at
home. It is not well, however, to burden the pupil with
the technical study of sounds; every teacher should have
some knowledge of theoretical phonetics, but should use
his knowledge with discrimination and remember that *what
is indispensable for the teacher is not always valuable for
the pupil.*

The importance of correct accentuation and correct syl-
lable-division should be early impressed upon the class.
The best way to avoid the false accentuation due to un-
conscious reproduction of the heavy English stress is to
insist that all syllables be accented equally, every word being pronounced syllable by syllable. The monotonous tone
which will result from such a practice will disappear in
the course of the first year. At its worst this monotonous

tone is preferable to the lively pronunciation often heard, fluent but vitiated by the strong English stress which can only with the greatest difficulty be shaken off when once it has become a habit. During the first year, fluency is the greatest foe to correct pronunciation.

The important rules governing pronunciation should be acquired gradually during the first semester, but when a pupil has once learned a rule he should *never* be allowed to neglect it; from the time, early in the semester, when he has learned the rule for the *e* in *venir* he must *never* be allowed to pronounce the word *vènir*. It is only by constant insistence, by inexorably stopping the student who has made such an error, wherever he may be, and however important the matter in hand may be, that a satisfactory pronunciation can be acquired.

The constant practice in pronunciation involved in the large amount of oral drill deemed advisable will not be sufficient; some time must be devoted to formal reading of the French, for reading and speaking bring into play different faculties, both of which must be utilized. A very little time, however, given to formal reading will adequately supplement the drill in pronunciation inherent in properly conducted oral work. It is well at times to have the whole class or parts of it read in concert in order to save time. This will not be difficult if pronunciation by syllables is insisted upon, and the teacher will be able to detect individual errors when pupils are taught to utter sounds distinctly.

The students in the end will acquire the pronunciation of the teacher, by the unescapable law of imitation sounding as the teacher does the vowels in *à* and *pas, peu* and *peur*, etc. Devices suggested here are intended to systematize the first steps and serve as a guide in the later work, supplemented at all times by imitation.

Every teacher should own a copy of Michaelis-Passy or the *International French-English Dictionary*, which give the pronunciation in phonetic transcription, and a complete manual such as Geddes', which has a valuable index and an excellent bibliography. But it would be exceedingly unwise to inflict upon the pupil all the subtle distinctions noted in these books, all three of which belong to the same "school" of pronunciation. In French, as in other languages, more than one pronunciation of some sounds is correct.

III

Conversation. The class in which a great deal of work is not done orally will almost inevitably lack life. Students will, of course, do a good deal of translation from English into French at home (see "Composition"). If possible, the teacher should correct and return all these exercises, but should this impose an intolerable burden upon him, he may select each day eight or ten to be corrected carefully, the rest to be gone over hurriedly and left unmarked. Ordinarily such correcting is done on the board during the recitation period, with the result that other important work is neglected. Correcting at the board is valuable and should not be entirely neglected, but two-thirds of the time spent in class on the correction of sentences written at home may profitably be devoted to oral work: the teacher reads the sentences, the pupils, with books closed, and papers put aside, translate into French. During the oral work the teacher should use the board freely to drive home corrections when they are of the sort that cannot be clearly understood unless written, and, in particular, to call attention to the most troublesome errors. It is difficult to find justification for the correction in class of work of this kind unless students are forbidden to open their exercise-books during the correction.

The retelling of matter studied previously, or just read by the teacher, is an excellent exercise which should be employed sparingly during the first year, but with increasing frequency after that.

These are the first steps toward conversation. As soon as possible, real conversation of an elementary type may be employed. The teacher should not do any more of the talking than necessary. Pupils should learn early to ask questions in French, as well as to answer them. Each pupil may be required to come to class provided with a question based on a given portion of the lesson, which another student is to be asked to answer: this is a good means of making the pupils do most of the talking.

At the end of the second year, pupils ought to be able to converse in French. Considerable grammatical inaccuracy in conversation (not in composition or oral drill) may be tolerated, as it is important for the pupil to gain confidence in himself and this he cannot do if he is interrupted at every moment.

The question how completely French should supplant English in the classroom is an exceedingly difficult one. In general it may be said that during the first year English must be used in explanations to the practical exclusion of French. Even in later years, much English must be used to clarify difficulties in translation, grammatical obscurities and the like. But toward the end of the second year, or earlier if possible, the teacher ought to make every effort to conduct the class as far as possible in French.

IV

Translation. In the matter of translation, accuracy must be insisted upon.

There is an unfortunate tendency at the present time to underrate the importance of translation; this is strange, considering the fact that in the long run it will probably be found that for the majority of students ability to translate is the most precious advantage gained from his study of French. In fact, pronunciation, composition and oral drill could hardly be justified if they did not serve as aids to translation, as well as possessing an intrinsic utility, practical and disciplinary. It would be unfortunate, indeed, if after his course the student were not able to translate French; it would be a matter for sincere congratulation if, in addition, he could write it, and still more emphatically if he could speak it. But the geographic position of the United States and our educational system make translation the paramount consideration. However, the old translation method of teaching is thoroughly discredited. Better results are attained when the language is treated as a living organism. Emphasis on oral drill and the use of a conversational vocabulary give life to the work, enable the student to talk and write French to the extent of his ability and afford him, again to the extent of his ability, that insight into the spirit of the language which is essential for thorough comprehension.

In the first two years *accurate translation* is the sign of *thorough comprehension.* After the first two years other tests of comprehension may be adopted, conversation and composition continuing to serve excellently for this purpose and being allowed, in addition, to become, more and more, ends in themselves.

Translation will prove of inestimable value, practical, disciplinary and cultural, to the pupil, if the teacher does not forget that meticulous accuracy is imperative. The pupil must be made to account for every word down to the smallest and least significant, and this from the first day of the first semester to the last day of the last semester. It is better to omit translation entirely than to allow the pupil to acquire slovenly habits in this, the most important phase of our work. It is not intended here to encourage the sort of translation which resolves itself into a pursuit of the nice distinctions between French and English idioms. Defects in English may be overlooked frequently if they arise from the evident desire of the student to fully express the idea conveyed in the French. Literal translation, even though it results in barbarous English, should not be frowned upon in the first year, for all too often by means of the so-called "free translation" the student hides his lack of accurate comprehension of the French. No translation should be accepted which does not show that the pupil *understands* the French. The classes are rare in which the pupils have been taught to recognize and reproduce correctly such elementary matters as tenses and articles. Here, as everywhere, elementary matters must be mastered before the student passes on to the more complicated. "Je vois un homme" *must* be translated "I see a man" and not, "I saw the man".

Pupils must be taught from the first day that looking up words in a vocabulary and stringing them on a cord is not translation, that the text carries a certain definite idea and that that idea máy be rendered in English as soon as the French is *fully* understood. In preparing his lesson the pupil should not look up a single word in the vocabulary and should not begin to translate until he has carefully read the sentence through to the end. An exercise of value is the reading by the teacher or by one of the pupils— the rest listening, books closed—of French prepared for translation.

After the first year so much will. be assigned for translation that it cannot all be gone over in class, nor will this be necessary if the intellectual conscience of the pupil has been sufficiently developed in so far as translation is concerned during the first year. The teacher will choose for translation significant passages and ascertain by judicious questioning whether the whole ground has been covered. Pupils should be able to retell in French in their own words the matter read.

Scrupulous exactness in translation betokening thorough comprehension of the French text is imperative.

V

Grammar. In connection with Conversation and Translation, as well as Composition, something should be said in regard to Grammar. The great fault of most of our textbooks is that they do not sufficiently distinguish essential and non-essential grammatical principles; this the teacher must do for himself. It is relatively easy to pick out the indispensable grammatical matter; let the teacher limit his efforts to this until it is learned, even if four years are required. It is unwise to expend much effort on difficulties such as the question of the preposition before an . infinitive ("je désire aller", "j'aime à aller", "je refuse d'aller") and the form of the pronoun in "je le fais écrire", "je lui fais écrire une lettre" before the many more important principles are *thoroughly* mastered. To spell the plural of "bijou" with an *s* and to say "du bon pain", are not serious blunders during the first year, or at any rate till there is no longer any danger of a pupil's using "chevals" as the plural of "cheval", and saying "j'ai pain" or "j'ai

de la pain" or "j'ai de pain". The rules for the agreement of participles are by no means so important as the
forms of the participles: until a pupil has not the slightest
inclination to say "j'ai vendé" he may be permitted to ig-
nore the question of agreement.

Here is a matter which demands the nicest discrimination on the part of the teacher, since, unfortunately, our
writers of grammars have not, for various reasons, done the
sifting for him.

Much grammatical matter may be treated as mere vocabulary and learned gradually as the student reads; for in-
stance, irregular adjectives, demonstrative and indefinite
pronouns, some irregular verb forms.

In the treatment of grammar one law must never be
forgotten: *practice is better than explanation.* The teacher
may spend too much time explaining a difficulty which can be
eliminated more easily by practice. If the partitive is being
treated, it is well to explain it briefly and then to give fifty
short sentences in which this construction is used: "he has
bread", "she has bread", "they have water", etc.

In this connection it may not be out of place to warn the
teacher that much valuable time may be wasted in answering
questions. Wide-awake students often come to class with a
sheaf of questions which they are eager to propound. It will
usually be found best to disregard most of these and to trust
to the exercise of the day and to practice to make everything
clear. Some time at the *end* of the recitation period may be
reserved for answering questions.

After a question has been put it is well for the teacher to
pause a moment before assigning it to any particular student,
so as to give all an opportunity to answer it mentally. The
pause may, however, easily be too long.

The teacher should know *very definitely* before coming to
class what work is to be done that day; he should be careful
not to spend time on interesting digressions, by talking too
much, or by allowing the pupils to talk too much. A recitation period is short and every minute must be usefully employed.

VI

The most important elements of instruction have been covered under the headings Pronunciation, Conversation, Translation. The following sections discuss subsidiary phases of the work which may be used to supplement the foregoing in the discretion of the teacher, but the danger of undue emphasis on purely secondary matter cannot be too strongly urged. Let us not forget that our most difficult problem is how to use the recitation period to best advantage; many exercises, excellent in themselves, must be omitted that the time to be devoted to essentials be not infringed upon.

The great question is not what to include, but what to exclude: let us never fail to discriminate primary and secondary matters.

VII

Composition. During the first year the grammar offers the necessary exercises.

During the second year original compositions may profitably be attempted, but the main effort should probably be made in connection with the text read in class: translation of simple English sentences composed by the teacher or furnished by the editor of the text. At the same time a more careful grammar review should be undertaken, lasting throughout the year. The book used may be the one covered in the first year or a more advanced one. In many cases sufficient composition work can be done in connection with the grammar review.

During the third and fourth years exercises based on the text read may be used or a separate composition book may be taken up, but more and more time ought to be devoted to original compositions.

Correction in class should be oral as far as possible.

Oral drill during the first year presupposes composition, the exercise in class being based on work previously written out by the pupil. In a less degree, the conversation of succeeding years may be based on compositions prepared beforehand by the class.

VIII

Outside Reading. Pupils are of varying ability. The teacher will find soon after the beginning of each year that a few of the pupils are able to do much more work than can be assigned to the class as a whole. It would be exceedingly unfortunate if the teacher did not devote special attention to these promising few. They should be encouraged in every way possible, in particular, by being given books to read at their leisure.

The better the exceptional pupil and the better the class, the more outside reading should be done. The ideal way of learning a language is by extensive reading, but this method is adapted only to the best students and to those who have received quite a different training from that which pupils receive in American schools today. The amount of outside reading covered may be regarded as a test of the ability of both teacher and pupil. In this work the teacher will ask the pupil to *look carefully at every word* and to try to get the sense of the passage without resorting to the vocabulary. The pupil should read much as he reads an English book with the important reservation that he should honestly endeavor to puzzle out every sentence before passing to the next.

In the choice of texts for this purpose, the teacher should endeavor to find material that is interesting and simpler than that being used in regular class work. Books and articles on art, history and the sciences may profitably be provided for students interested in a special field.

IX

Sight Reading. Sight reading is of value in itself and also because it may well be utilized to vary the regular program of the recitation. The amount to be covered will be determined by the capacity of the class. It will be well to have the books used for this purpose left in the classroom ready for use at any time. The text used in the regular work may be used for sight reading, translation continuing after the assignment for the day has been adequately covered.

There will be no occasion for sight reading during the first year; in succeeding years more and more may be done.

X

Memorizing. This work is exceedingly valuable. Any simple prose, even that of no intrinsic value, may be chosen for the purpose, but nothing is better than La Fontaine's fables, despite the occasional solecisms of vocabulary and expression. The amount of memorizing that can be profitably attempted depends entirely upon the ease with which the class does it. If pupils memorize quickly, they can hardly do too much, if they memorize with very great difficulty, they had better do none at all.

Short sentences or phrases important in that they illustrate grammatical principles may well be culled from grammar or reading, and kept in a notebook to be reviewed until they are known by heart.

XI

Dictation. Dictation is of unquestionable value in controlling auditory exactness, but the teacher will find little or no time to devote to it.

XII

Choice of Texts. The typical American student reads voluntarily nothing but "interesting" stories and dramas. So firmly fixed is this predilection that it will be unwise for the teacher to fail at any time to recognize it. But, valuable as the study of French is for commercial and other practical reasons, we should never forget that its real justification for the finer type of boy and girl lies in its cultural associations. Therefore, wherever it is possible, works of real literature should be read. In the outline offered below, practically nothing of high literary merit is listed under the first and second years; but during the third and fourth years, class reading should be restricted to works of genuine literary value.

After the second year, increasing attention should be paid to French literature and French history.

XIII

French Life, Literature and History. Articles on France appearing in current American periodicals, such as the National Geographical Magazine, should be brought to the attention of the class. Important French festivals and birthdays of famous Frenchmen may be made the subject of compositions or conversations. Too much time, however, may easily be spent on these matters and it well to remember always that the primary object of the high school course is to impart a knowledge of the language. Yet, something of French history and of the history of French literature should certainly be acquired during the third and fourth years.

XIV

Cercle Français. It is highly desirable that a French club be formed of advanced pupils, to meet if possible once a week. Recitations, songs, games, dialogues, charades, dramatizations of La Fontaine, and similar activities may make up the evening's entertainment. Occasionally a pupil or the teacher may give a talk on a subject concerning French literature, history or life. Short plays may be presented. It should not be forgotten that the memorizing of parts in a play is an excellent exercise.

The following one-act plays are suitable for the purpose:

Augier: *Le Post-scriptum.*

H. Bataille: *La Déclaration.*

T. Bernard: *L'Anglais tel qu'on le parle.*
Le Peintre exigeant.

Brieux: *L'Ecole des belles-mères.*

Courteline: *La Paix chez soi.*
Le Gendarme est sans pitié.
Le Commissaire est bon enfant.
Un Client sérieux.

A. France: *La Comédie de celui qui épousa une femme muette.*

Mme. de Girardin: *La Joie fait peur.*

Labiche: *La Grammaire.*
    Le Voyage de Monsieur Perrichon.
    La Poudre aux yeux.
    Le Misanthrope et l'Auvergnat.
    La Lettre chargée.
    La Cigale chez les fourmis.
Meilhac et Halévy: *L'Eté de la Saint-Martin.*
Moinaux: *Les Deux Sourds.*
Musset: *Il faut qu'une porte soit ouverte ou fermée.*
    Un Caprice.
(See also Oliver, *Suggestions and References*, p. 61).

XV

The Classroom. There should be in the classroom:
1. A map of France.
2. Pictures of French men,, monuments and scenes.
3. A library. It is not possible to select a library which would suit the varied needs and means of schools, but certain books are essential: a good French-English and English-French dictionary and the *Petit Larousse illustré* or the *Larousse pour tous*. In addition it will be well to have as many texts as possible and other books selected from the list of Material for Reference and Occasional Use offered here below.

XVI

University Textbook Library. Many of the books and other material in the list here appended have been collected in the University Textbook Library and most of the rest will be added as soon as possible. Teachers are invited to inspect this library and may have any book sent to them through their local library. They are reminded that all American publishers willingly send books for examination.

OUTLINÉ OF THE FOUR YEAR COURSE

Teachers are urged to provide themselves with the following excellent bibliographical manual: Thomas Edward Oliver, *Suggestions and References for Modern Language Teachers*, second edition, University of Illinois School of Education, Bulletin No. 18, Urbana, Illinois (price 25 cents).

They should also have on hand the catalogues of the following publishers:

Allyn and Bacon, 172 Tremont St., Boston; 1006 So. Michigan Ave., Chicago.

American Book Co., 100 Washington Sq., New York; 1104 So. Wabash Ave., Chicago.

D. Appleton and Co., 35 West 32nd St., New York; 2457 Prairie Ave., Chicago.

E. P. Dutton and Co., 681 Fifth Ave., New York. [Collection Gallia.]

Ginn and Co., 29 Beacon St., Boston; 2301–2311 Prairie Ave., Chicago.

D. C. Heath and Co., 231–245 West 39th St., New York; 623–633 So. Wabash Ave., Chicago.

Henry Holt and Co., 19 West 44th St., New York; 623 So. Wabash Ave., Chicago.

W. R. Jenkins Co., 6th Ave. at 48th St., New York.

The Macmillan Co., 64–66 Fifth Ave., New York.

Thos. Nelson and Sons, 681 Fourth Ave., New York. [Collection Nelson.]

Oxford University Press, American Branch, 35 West 32nd St., New York.

Benj. H. Sanborn and Co., 623 So. Wabash Ave., Chicago.

Scott, Foresman and Co., 623–633 So. Wabash Ave., Chicago.

Charles Scribner's Sons, 597 Fifth Ave., New York.

Silver, Burdett and Co., 126 Fifth Ave., New York.

Books from abroad may be purchased through Schoenhof Book Co., 128 Tremont St., Boston, and G. E. Stechert and Co., 151–155 West 25th St., New York.

FIRST YEAR

Grammar:

Chardenal's *Complete French Course* (Allyn and Bacon)

First semester: lessons 1–30.

Second semester: lessons 31–69.

Fraser and Squair's *French Grammar* (the complete form)
(Heath)

First semester: lessons 1–23 (with omissions in 17–23, insistence only on the most important grammatical principles).

Second semester: finish first part (with many omissions, insistence only on the most important grammatical principles).

Méras, *Le Premier Livre* and *Le Second Livre* (American Book Co.)

First semster: 35 lessons of *Le Premier Livre.*

Second semester: remaining lessons of *Le Premier Livre* and 35 lessons in *Le Second Livre.*

Supplementary (30–100 pages):

Ballard: *Short Stories for Oral French* (Scribner)

François: *Easy French-Reading* (Holt)

François and Giroud: *Simple-French* (Holt)

Guerber: *Contes et légendes* (American Book Company)

Lazare: *Les Plus Jolis Contes de fées* (Ginn)

Mairet: *La Tâche du petit Pierre* (American Book Company)

Méras and Roth: *Petits Contes de France* (American Book Company)

SECOND YEAR

Grammar:

Review of work done in first year.

Reading (about 200 pages):

Assollant: *Récits de la vieille France* (Heath)

Bornier: *La Lizardière* (Holt)

Bruce: *Contes de la guerre de 1870* (Holt)

Erckmann-Chatrian: *Le Juif polonais* (Heath)

Foa: *Le Petit Robinson de Paris* (American Book Company)

Halévy: *L'Abbé Constantin* (Allyn and Bacon)
          Contes choisis (Holt)
La Bedollière: *La Mére Michel et son chat* (American Book
          Company)
Labiche: *La Grammaire*
           La Poudre aux yeux
           Le Voyage de M. Perrichon
de la Brète: *Mon Oncle et mon curé*
La Fontaine: *Fables*
Malot: *Sans Famille*

Supplementary:
Bierman and Frank: *Conversational French Reader* (Allyn
          and Bacon)
Giese and Cerf: *Simplest Spoken French* (Holt)

Outside Reading (about 150 pages):
About: *Le Roi des montagnes*
Claretie: *Pierrille* (Holt)
Dumas: *La Tulipe noire*
         Le Comte de Monte-Cristo
         Les Trois Mousquetaires
Erckmann-Chatrian: *Madame Thérèse*
Feuillet: *Le Roman d'un jeune homme pauvre*
Theuriet: *L'Abbé Daniel* (Holt)

Sight-Reading (about 30 pages):
Moffett: *Récits historiques* (Heath)
Muller: *Les Grandes Découvertes modernes* (Heath)
Talbot: *Le Français et sa patrie* (Sanborn)
Weill: *French Historical Reader* (American Book Company)

THIRD AND FOURTH YEAR

Grammar review.

Composition:
François: *Introductory French Prose Composition* (Ameri-
          can Book Company)
Levi: *French Composition* (Holt)

Conversation:

Pattou: *Causeries en France* (Heath)

Sight Reading (50–100 pages each year):
The books mentioned under second year and
Canfield: *French Lyrics* (Holt)
La Fontaine: *Fables*
and other books mentioned below.

THIRD YEAR

Reading (about 300 pages):
Bazin: *Les Oberlé*
Canfield: *French Lyrics* (Holt)   .
Coppée: *Le Luthier de Crémone* (Allyn and Bacon)
Daudet: *Contes*
France: *Le Livre de mon ami* (Holt)
Henning: *French Lyrics of the Nineteenth Century* (Ginn)
Hugo: *Quatre-vingt-treize.*
Labiche: *Moi* (Allyn and Bacon)
La Fontaine: *Fables*
Lamartine: *Jeanne d'Arc*
Loti: *Le Roman d'un enfant* (Heath)
Mérimée: *Colomba*
　　　　Carmen (Ginn)
　　　　Quatre Contes (Holt)
Molière: *Le Bourgeois gentilhomme*
　　　　Le Médecin malgré lui •
Sand: *La Mare au Diable*
　　　La Petite Fadette

Outside Reading (about 400 pages)
The books mentioned under second year and
Daudet: *Le Petit Chose*
Hugo: *Cosette* (Oxford)
　　　Gavroche (Oxford)
Verne: *Le Tour du monde en 80 jours*
　　　20,000 Lieues sous les mers

FOURTH YEAR

Reading (about 400 pages):
The books mentioned under third year and
Augier:　*Le Gendre de Monsieur Poirier*
Balzac:　*Eugénie Grandet*
　　　　　Stories (Holt)
Bornier:　*La Fille de Roland*
Corneille:　*Le Cid*
Daudet:　*Tartarin de Tarascon*
　　　　　La Belle-Nivernaise
Hugo:　*Hernani*
Loti:　*Pêcheur d'Islande*
　　　　Ramuntcho
Maupassant:　*Contes*
Molière:　*L'Avare*
　　　　　Le Malade imaginaire
　　　　　Les Précieuses ridicules
Musset:　*Poems and Plays* (Ginn)
Pailleron:　*Le Monde où l'on s'ennuie*
Racine:　*Athalie*
　　　　Phédre
Renan:　*Ma Soeur Henriette* (Holt)
Taine:　*L'Ancien Régime* (Heath)
de Vigny:　*La Canne de jonc*
Voltaire:　*Zadig* (Heath)

Outside Reading (about 500 pages):
The books mentioned under second year and the following:
France:　*Le Crime de Sylvestre Bonnard*
Hugo:　*Les Misérables*
Sand:　*Mauprat* (Nelson)
Sarcey:　*Le Siége de Paris* (Heath)

Material for Reference and Occasional Use

DICTIONARIES

Edgren and Burnet:　*French-English and English-French*
　　　(Holt $1.50; indicates derivations)
Elwall:　*French-English and English-French*, 2 vols. (Stechert, $4)

Gasc: *French-English and English-French* (Holt, $1.50)

Heath: *French-English and English-French* (Heath, $1.50)

Hatzfeld-Darmesteter-Thomas: *Dictionnaire de la Langue française*. 2 vols. (the standard dictionary, Paris, Delagrave, $7)

International French-English and English-French (indicates pronunciation), $3. Hinds and Noble.

Petit Larousse illustré (Paris, Larousse, $1.50)

Larousse pour tous, 2 vols. (Paris, Larousse, $10)

GRAMMAR

Augé: *Cours de grammaire*, 4 vols. (Paris, Larousse, $2.50)

PRONUNCIATION

Cerf: *Essentials of French Pronunciation* (Holt, 25c)

Churchman: *An Introduction to the Pronunciation of French* (Jenkins, 50c)

Geddes: *French Pronunciation* (Oxford, 75c)

Michaelis-Passy: *Dictionnaire phonétique de la langue française* (exclusively a dictionary of pronunciation using the alphabet of the "Association Phonétique Internationale"; Paris, Le Soudier, $2)

Nitze and Wilkins: *A Handbook of French Phonetics* (Holt, 40c)

Nyrop: *Manuel phonétique du français parlé* (Paris, Picard, $1.25)

VERBS, IDIOMS, VOCABULARY

Armstrong: *Syntax of the French Verb* (Holt, 90c)

Billaudeau: *Collection of French Idioms, Sayings and Proverbs with their French Equivalents* (Stechert, $2.50)

Bossert et Beljame: *Les Mots anglais groupés d'après le sens* (Paris, Hachette, 40c)

Guibillon: *La France*, French Life and Ways, ed. W. Ripman (Dutton, $1)

Marchand: *Four Thousand French Idioms and Proverbs* (Brentano, $1.25)

Meadmore: *Les Idiotismes et les proverbes anglais* (Paris, Hachette, 40c)

Spiers: *Notebook of Modern Languages* (Heath, 25c)

Tricoche: *Stumbling Blocks of the French Language* (Park Place, Morristown, N. J. 75c)1

HISTORY AND MONUMENTS

Adams: *The Growth of the French Nation* (Macmillan, $1.25)

Bracq: *France under the Republic* (Scribner, $1.50)

Duruy: *Histoire de France*, 2 vols. (Paris, Hachette, $2.50; in English translation in Everyman's Library, 2 vols. Dutton, 40c a vol.)

Fallex et Mairey: *La France et ses colonies au début du XXe siècle* (Paris, Delagrave, $1)

Guérard: *French Civilization in the Nineteenth Century* (The Century Co., $3)

Bournon: *Paris-Atlas* (Paris, Larousse, $5)

Atlas Larousse illustré (première partie: La France et ses colonies (Paris, Larousse, $4)

Histoire de France illustrée, 2 vol. (Paris, Larousse, $14)

Histoire de France contemporaine, 1871–1913, (Larousse, $8)

LITERATURE

Abry, Audic, Crouzet: *Histoire illustrée de la littérature française* (Paris, Didier, $1.50)

Dowden: *French Literature* (Appleton, $1.50)

Strowski: *Tableau de la littérature française au XIXe siècle* (Paris, Delaplane, $1)

Wright: *History of French Literature*, (Oxford, $3)

FRENCH LIFE AND IDEALS

Brownell: *French Traits* (Scribner, $1.50)

Hamerton: *Round my House* (Little, Brown, $1.50)

C. Johnson: *Along French Byways* (Macmillan, $1.50)

Klein: *An American Student in France* (McClurg, $2.50)

Lynch: *French Life in Town and Country* (Putnam, $1.20)

Wendell: *France of Today* (Scribner, $1)

Science and Learning in France (McClurg, $1)

MAPS

Nouveau Paris monumental (Paris, Garnier, 50c)
Levasseur: *Carte murale de la France* (Paris, Delagrave, $5)
Levasseur: *Carte murale de l'Europe* (Paris, Delagrave, $5)

WALL-PICTURES FOR CONVERSATION

Walter-Ballard: *Wall-pictures* (Scribner, $2.75 for the set of
three)

SONGS

Carter: *Petit Recueil de chants français* (Oxford, large edition, words and music, $1.50; small edition, without
music, 50c)
Gay: *Chansons: Poésies et jeux français* (Jenkins, 50c)
Walter-Ballard: *French Songs* (Scribner, 50c)

GAMES

Ernst: *French Conversation Cards* (Jenkins, 50c)
Perrot: *J'apprends les langues vivantes en jouant* (2 series,
Jenkins, 50c each)
Dutoit: *Jeu illustré* (Jenkins, 50c)

BOOKS FOR TRAVELERS

Bellows: *Dictionary for the Pocket* (Holt, $2.55)
New French Conversation Dictionary (London, Jaschke, 75c)
Murray's Handbook of Travel Talk (Scribner, $1.25)
  The *Guides Joanne* (Paris, Hachette) are the standard
French tourist guides. They are in various forms at various
prices, ranging from monographs on single cities and regions
at 10c to 20c to *Grands Guides* at $2.00)

BOOKS FOR SOLDIERS

The above and

Giese and Cerf: *Simplest Spoken French* (Holt, 55c)

Vizetelly: *Soldier's Service Dictionary* (Funk and Wagnalls, $1)

Wilkins and Coleman: *Army French* (University of Chicago Press, 40c)

Willcox: *A French-English Military Technical Dictionary* (Harper, $4)

PERIODICALS

Les Annales politiques et littéraires (weekly, Paris, $5 a year; of periodicals here enumerated probably the best adapted to high school use.)

L'Echo des deux mondes (monthly, Chicago, $2 a year)

Journal de l'Université des Annales (fortnightly, Paris, $3 a year)

Larousse mensuel illustré (monthly, encyclopedic, Paris, Larousse, $2.50 a year)

L'Opinion (political and literary, weekly, Paris, $6 per year)

Qui-pourquoi-comment? L'Encyclopédie de la Jeunesse (Paris, Larousse, $2 per year)

NEWSPAPERS

The best Paris newspapers are *Le Temps* and *Le Journal des Débats.*

Le Courrier des Etats-Unis (New York; daily $12.60 a year, daily except Sunday $10.00, Sunday $2.50 a year, weekly edition $5.20 a year. The weekly edition, supplemented if possible, by the Sunday edition, which is entirely distinct, furnishes satisfactorily the current news.)

BOOKS ON SCIENTIFIC AND TECHNICAL SUBJECTS

Tolhausen: *Technological Dictionary: English-German-French* (Macmillan, $2.75)

Tolhausen: *Dictionnaire technologique: Français-Allemand-Anglais* (Macmillan, $2.75)

Cambon: *La France au travail.* 6 vols. (Paris, Roger, $1 a vol.)

Daniels: *French Scientific Reader* (Oxford, $1.75)

Dike: *Scientific French Reader* (Silver, Burdett, $1)

Jago: *La France qui travaille* (Heath, 50c)

COMMERCIAL

Graham and Oliver: *French Commercial Practice* (Macmillan, 2 parts at $1)

Graham and Oliver: *The Foreign Trader's Correspondence Handbook* (Macmillan, $1)

PERIODICAL ON SCIENTIFIC SUBJECTS

La Nature (weekly, Paris, $5.50)

TEXTS OF FRENCH LITERATURE

It is desirable to have on the shelves of the reference library, to encourage outside reading on the part of pupils, as many as possible of the texts of French literature published in America for use in schools.

The following series of masterpieces of French literature are recommended:

Auteurs français (editions for class use in France, Paris, Hachette, about $1 per vol.)

Bibliothèque Larousse (Paris, Larousse, 40c per vol.)

Collection Gallia (New York, Dutton, 40c per vol.)

Collection Nelson (Nelson, New York, 40c per vol.)

Les Meilleurs Auteurs classiques français et étrangers (Paris, Flammarion, 40c per vol.)

Pages choisies des grands écrivains (Paris, Colin, $1 per vol.)

Catalogues of these series may be had from the Schoenhof Book Co., and G. E. Stechert and Co.

CPSIA information can be obtained
at www.ICGtesting.com
Printed in the USA
BVHW071619280119
538839BV00028B/2414/P